"You cannot imagine what
it was like for a poor lad
like me going into one
of these houses. It was
like going into a palace,
everything around was
so rich and beautiful.
But what was strange
was that the front doors
were always unlocked."

Ernie Mason, A Working Man

BEHIND THE FAÇADE

Archives Alive

QueenSpark Books was formed in 1972 and has published over 110 books on Brighton and Hove that chronicle the city's social history across the past 100 years, in people's own words. We have a unique archive of fascinating and important information, and Archives Alive – a project funded by The National Lottery Heritage Fund – makes these stories accessible again.

Behind the Façade – The terraced communities of Brighton & Hove is one of four Archives Alive books published by QueenSpark Books in July 2019. It has been edited and produced by volunteers. With guidance from industry professionals, the volunteer editors chose a theme to explore, and selected content from QueenSpark's online archive and elsewhere.

Other volunteers researched photographic sites for images to accompany the text. Editors selected photographs and worked with designers on layout and design of the books.

Archives Alive also enabled volunteers to identify old documents, slides and letters. This material improves access to heritage material via our website and is permanently deposited at The Keep for public accessibility. www.thekeep.info

In 2019-2020, we are engaging communities across the city, using Archives Alive books to stimulate reading and as a starting point for conversations about our shared heritage. We hope those discussions lead to more stories being told – and that QueenSpark Books publishes people's reflections for many years to come.

We are very grateful to all of our volunteers, who have worked incredibly hard to make this historical material new, and relevant again.

Please enjoy.

QueenSpark Books

Introduction

We were able to interrogate the QueenSpark archives and others to see what we could learn about how the city has developed since its inception. Our team of editors chose to focus on terraced housing. We looked at how this particular architectural construct influenced the everyday living of individual lives whilst also fashioning the communities that thrived within them.

Terraces are a common feature of urban design throughout British towns and cities. Brighton & Hove is no different, but we were struck by the close proximity of the grand terraces, built to master plans, and the standard working-class terraces, thrown up as quickly and cheaply as possible.

The grand designs of Kemptown and Brunswick were conceived to be elegant and appealing to the affluent classes. Kemptown was the ambitious and costly scheme of Thomas Kemp, an MP in nearby Lewes, who was aiming to entice the highest echelons of society.

On the other side of the city, Brunswick Town, now simply called Brunswick, was founded by the Rev. Thomas Scutt and designed by Charles Busby following his involvement in the development of Kemptown. He chose a name that patrons would have associated with the royal family, intrinsically linking his building scheme with upper-class fashionable life.

Yet geographically these ambitious developments became surrounded by typical two-up two-down terrace designs, so characteristic of many industrial Victorian towns. This housing was built to provide high-density accommodation for the working-class, the plan being to pack as many dwellings into the space as was possible. In some areas of central Brighton and Hanover, these terraces became so dilapidated they were declared slum dwellings and were ultimately demolished.

This change created social tiers in the city as areas became defined by their terraces. Experiences within these two worlds were very different. As we read through the archives, we found some recollections that dealt directly with living conditions and problems that inhabitants encountered. These included unethical landlords who left tenants to deal with bed bug or cockroach infestations, or cases where damp became so bad the plaster would fall from the bedroom walls. Other recollections revealed information by omission, for example, talking about leisure activities outside the house, because there was not enough room inside for siblings to all play together.

These stories came predominantly from the working-class terraces, where the fabric of the house itself was woven into everyday life. The close proximity of neighbours either sharing a house, or those who lived adjacent, made it impossible for families to maintain privacy. People remember those who experienced the same hardships, for example, a reliance on the local pawnbroker who became an important and regular feature. This circumstance created small communities in which people supported each other both practically and emotionally.

By contrast, those living in the grand terraces of Kemptown or Brunswick maintained a distance from their neighbours. Recollections from these properties come predominantly from visitors or employees remembering the impact the buildings had on them when they arrived. Running such large and costly houses took a considerable workforce, and recollections are almost exclusively made up from those who served rather than by their employers. It is interesting that although they were built as houses, these terraces are depicted as places of employment and not as tangible homes.

The terraces of Brighton & Hove offered an architectural structure for the lives of those who built the city. Families lived, worked and died in these terraces, and provided each other with support and camaraderie, and the extracts included in this book epitomise those experiences. We found them to be nostalgic and reminiscent of an old Brighton that has perhaps been forgotten, but people are still finding communities here that will welcome them and to which they can belong. And reading through these recollections, it is very clear why.

Jenny O'Donoghue, Diana Varadi and James Woolley
Editors – *Behind the Façade*
July 2019

1: BRIGHTON & HOVE
EARLY DEVELOPMENT

Development

In the early 1800s Hove was just a small village surrounded by farmland, and Brighton, which had flourished, had hit such hard times that in the 1720s it was dismissed by Daniel Defoe as "a poor fishing town, old built and at the very edge of the sea".

A new phase in Brighton's development began as the economy recovered after the Napoleonic wars. By the early 1820s the economy had improved and a national building boom was apparent, allowing many opportunities for speculation. In Brighton, the landowners Thomas Read Kemp and the Rev. Thomas Scutt seized the opportunity to produce grand schemes which could compete with Nash's developments in the capital and turn Brighton into an elegant "London by the sea".

Both Brunswick Town in Hove, and Kemp Town[1] in Brighton, were such developments. They offered high quality houses which were expected to appeal to courtiers, those on the periphery of court circles and successful Brighton professionals and entrepreneurs. During the next twenty years the Brunswick and Kemp Town developments did attract top aristocracy including most of the British Cabinet and many European royals. [2]

"Nothing shows more clearly the rapid rise of the middle class in England than the contrast of the accommodation which suited the citizens of London seventy or eighty years ago, and that now demanded by their sons and grandsons. Middle Street and Russell Street sufficed for the one, Brunswick Square and Terrace, Palmeira Square and the palatial mansions of West Brighton can scarcely suffice for the other!" [3]

Hove, which still retains nearly its ancient name, being written in the Domesday Book 'How', is termed the younger sister of Brighton, and has continued to grow by her side from an infant-like village into a large, prosperous, and fashionable

(1) Please see editors' note, chapter 2, on the use of Kemp Town / Kemptown.
(2) The Regency Town House, www.rth.org
(3) The Book of Brighton As It Was and As It Is by Chas. H. Ross.

town. "A few years since," I read, "a person might have stood in the field which then ran from the top of Brunswick Place to Chatfield's Farm, and looking towards the west, have seen at a distance of a mile or two the neat and unpretending church, with the village lying to the southward of old Hove. All between were green fields, dotted here and there with a house or farm, &c., but which offered little interruption to the view of spectator. At the present time the aspect and condition of this vast area is entirely changed. From the village has sprung a town – a town of magnificence – inhabited by the wealthy of the land. The population of Hove at the beginning of the century was 100; in the year 1831, 1,360; and ten years later it had increased to 2,509. In 1878 the population stood at 17,587, the number of houses being 2,432, and the rateable value £144,058." [4]

Image 1

The Regency Period [...] For many years Brighton had been the resort of fashion, the sea front of the town for carriages went no further westward than a tumble-down public house called The Ship in Distress, at the corner of Middle Street. The houses lining

(Image 1) Plan of Brighton and its environs, 1837. Royal Pavilion & Museums.
(4) The Book of Brighton As It Was and As It Is by Chas. H. Ross.

the road before 1822 would seem to have been of small value, and even a year after the road was opened the lease of No. 53 was sold for £150. When the lease next ran out, Mr. Bishop says it was bought for £2,300.

The Brighton of the Regency was, after all, but a poor, shabby, shambling sort of place, as you may see for yourself any day you like to look at the pictures in the Pavilion. But it is not of the past I would just now speak, but of the incomparable King's Road, at the present time the grandest promenade in all the world. I cannot forgive my ancestors, the Ancient Britons, for one thing. What were they muddling about when they chose the site for London where they did, and how was it Julius Caesar and the other Roman gentlemen who dropped in uninvited and stayed to a tea or two did not set things right? Of course Brighton ought to have been the capital. There is one thing, though, that tends somewhat to console me. If this amazing thoroughfare be not actually in London at the present moment, all London seems to be promenading in it. Why, this gloriously bright afternoon you cannot walk five yards, if you keep your eyes open, without seeing some nobility. [5]

~~~~~~~~~

Leisure destination

Brighton has always been a bustling seaside town, and hosting day-trippers from London as well as visitors from the continent became part and parcel of everyday life, providing gainful employment in hotels, as well as offering an extra revenue stream to those with initiative.

~~~~~~~~~

Railways

It was the opening of the railway in the 1840s which ultimately changed the character of both Brighton & Hove. At first, the new mode of travel attracted affluent visitors in even greater numbers, leading to particularly glittering social seasons in the late 1840s, but, as the railway companies began to offer cheaper tickets and excursions, these attracted new types of travellers. Brighton found popularity with working-class day-

(5) The Book of Brighton As It Was and As It Is by Chas. H. Ross.

trippers from London whilst Hove attracted the suburban middle classes and Victorian commuters. [6]

Image 2

Piers

As daylight went, the sounds were on the seafront road and piers. The steamer docking at the end of the pier would glow with lights. There were three such paddle boats which operated from Brighton: *Waverley*, *Devonia* and *Brighton Belle*. These gave trips to France as well as along our coastal strip. [7]

Image 3

(Image 2) Hove Railway Station, 1896. James Gray Collection.
(Image 3) Paddle steamer, mooring at the West Pier landing stage, Brighton, 1930s. Royal Pavilion & Museums.
(6) The Regency Town House.
(7) QueenSpark Special Supplement.

The popularity of the Chain Pier – built in 1823 – inspired a group of local investors to engage an experienced pier engineer, Eugenius Birch, to design an entirely new pier at the western end of Brighton.

The Pier took three years to build and was opened to the public with great celebrations on 6th October 1866.

The Pier, at first called the New Pier, soon became known as the West Pier. The toll of 2d was enough to deter most poorer people from entering. Entertainment was provided by military bands; there were deckchairs and kiosks sold refreshments and such items as silhouettes. The Pier became a fashionable place to see and be seen – early pictures show people walking up and down it in all their finery, breathing in the fresh sea air. [8]

Bath chairs & carriages

Sometimes, on fine days, an old boy in a bowler hat would trundle down a thing on four wheels, two large at the back and two small ones in the front, which looked like a miniature horse cab.

He would pull it over the Front, then shunt it back and forth

(Image 4) Illustration of Brighton's Chain Pier. Royal Pavilion & Museums
(8) Oh! What a Lovely Pier by Daphne Mitchell.

14

behind me, until it was on the Rank and it looked like he was plying for hire.

It was a bath chair. Not an ordinary bath chair, this one was licensed by the Council and coach built. It had a lovely leather hood made exactly like the horse cab hoods, able to go up and down, a leather sheet that buttoned up each side to protect the passenger from dust, etc., a rug to wrap round the person's feet and legs, a footstool for them to rest their feet on and to get in and out.

The body was real coach built, just like a cab, nicely painted, dried and varnished. In fact a human drawn, one seater, hackney carriage.

They were mostly pulled by old horse cab drivers, several by old army and navy men, one by an old retired ex-Indian railway engine driver, and another by an old Canadian bloke who had stopped here after the First World War. [9]

A short distance away was a transport for the not so young. I think they were called Victoria Carriages, where the passengers sat high on an upholstered seat, complete with cushions and travel rug. A man would pull this along at a slow pace, while under her sunshade madam would enjoy the sea air. The ladies riding in these seemed very aloof. They took no notice of anyone, and less of the human being acting as a horse, to give her enjoyment. [10]

~~~~~~~~~~~

Dereliction and housing shortages

Despite the economic boom enjoyed by the successful seaside town, during the middle of the twentieth century many buildings had been left derelict and there was a chronic housing crisis in the city. The fashionable quarters of the city, with the splendours of the grand terraces, became neglected. It was the dedication of local residents clamouring for change that saved this beautiful architecture and helped provide solutions for some of the city's poorest inhabitants.

(9) Hard Times and Easy Terms by Bert Healey.
(10) QueenSpark Special Supplement.

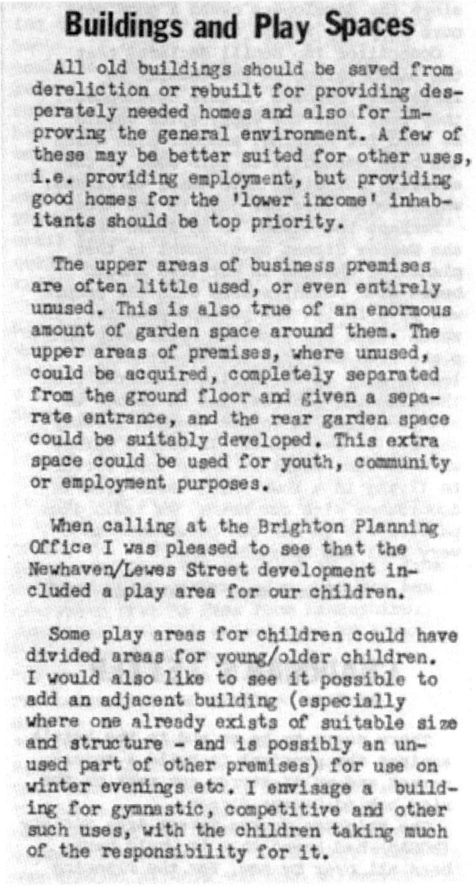

Buildings and Play Spaces

All old buildings should be saved from dereliction or rebuilt for providing desperately needed homes and also for improving the general environment. A few of these may be better suited for other uses, i.e. providing employment, but providing good homes for the 'lower income' inhabitants should be top priority.

The upper areas of business premises are often little used, or even entirely unused. This is also true of an enormous amount of garden space around them. The upper areas of premises, where unused, could be acquired, completely separated from the ground floor and given a separate entrance, and the rear garden space could be suitably developed. This extra space could be used for youth, community or employment purposes.

When calling at the Brighton Planning Office I was pleased to see that the Newhaven/Lewes Street development included a play area for our children.

Some play areas for children could have divided areas for young/older children. I would also like to see it possible to add an adjacent building (especially where one already exists of suitable size and structure - and is possibly an unused part of other premises) for use on winter evenings etc. I envisage a building for gymnastic, competitive and other such uses, with the children taking much of the responsibility for it.

Image 5

~~~~~~~

Squatting

Amanda Tudor Williams and her son Toby have moved into an empty house in Quebec Street. The landlord had been letting it fall apart, and they desperately needed somewhere to live. The Sussex Housing Movement, a squatting movement which is committed to finding accommodation for homeless people in houses which have been left empty for years, helped them to move in. They hope the "legal warning" in the window of their home will ward off evictors. [11]

(Image 5) Excerpt from front cover, QueenSpark Newsletter, Issue 23, Summer 1979.
(11) QueenSpark Newsletter, Issue 32, Summer 1984.

Council house waiting lists

Did You Know?

- That there are 370,000 construction workers unemployed in Britain.
- That there are around 3,000 people on the Brighton Housing Waiting List.
- That the prospect for Council house building is negative.

COUNCIL HOUSING WAITING LIST, 1 JAN-31 MAR. 1981

Housing Waiting List	1,232
PLUS	
Families in Condemned Property	18
Awaiting rehousing from current stage Whitehawk development	73
New applications since 1 Jan.	195
Requiring transfer to warden accom.	92
Needing transfer to different size accomodation	1,216
Awaiting Sheltered accomodation	198
" " accom.-transfers	92
Families in Bed and Breakfast	60

(57 of the families in B&B were on the housing list before becoming homeless and have thus lived in Brighton for over three years.)

Image 6

Oriental Place

Three years ago, I was commissioned by Brighton Housing Trust to photograph The Regency Hotel in Oriental Place, Brighton. It has, for the past thirty years, been run as a private concern, housing the city's homeless. In 2002 the housing trust purchased the property and began a major restoration project. My role has been to document the entire process and the lives of those affected, the residents, staff and workmen, as the place embarked on a new episode in its life.

(Image 6) Excerpt from back cover, QueenSpark Newsletter, Issue 28, Spring-Summer 1981.

The Grade II listed building was built in the early 19th century as part of the city's grand Regency vision. It started life as four individual dwellings which were used as lodging houses. Between the wars, they were combined into a single hotel. In the mid-1960s it was established as the country's first YWCA and, in 1980, it became a hostel for homeless men. On my arrival, the building was in an appalling state – virtually uninhabitable. There were, nevertheless, still sixty residents, many of whom remained throughout the reconstruction period.

I photographed the inhabitants as well as spaces and surfaces and everyday objects. The images bear witness to past events and catch the traces of the lives that have been spent here – the lives of those that have known homely comforts, style and grace and also those that have suffered abuse, aggression and despair. Maybe now, with the restoration, will come lives that know hope.

I have tried to uncover the things that have been hidden by time or social invisibility, to show the tensions that are inherent in a place such as this and reveal the relationship in which this dwelling and its inhabitants have been enmeshed. [12]

(Image 7 opposite) Brighthelmston, 1779. Royal Pavilion & Museums.
(12) Roofless, The Regency Project, by Richard Rowland.

References
A. The Theater
B. Lady Huntington's Chapel
C. Quakers Meeting
D. Presbyterian Meeting
E.F. Free Schools
G. Custom House
H. Post Office
I. The Bank
K. Castle Tavern
L. Old Ship Tavern

Road to LONDON by J.F.T

North Row

NORTH STREET

WEST STREET

MIDDLE STREET

EAST STREET

SHIP STREET

THE STEYNE

A very fine Sand dry at Low Water

Scale of a quarter of a Mile or Twenty Chains

2: GRAND TERRACES OF KEMPTOWN

~~~~~~

Editors' note: The names Kemp Town and Kemptown
can be used interchangeably. *Behind the Façade* utilizes both
versions in accordance with source materials.

Kemptown terraces

Kemp Town – also known as Kemptown – was developed on the eastern edge of the city in the name of its visionary, Thomas Read Kemp (1782-1844). He commissioned Charles Busby and Amon Wilds – renowned architects, and builders, in the Regency period – to create the estate. Elegant terraces, now Grade I listed buildings, were designed to establish Brighton as a destination for wealthy patrons and to provide luxurious living.

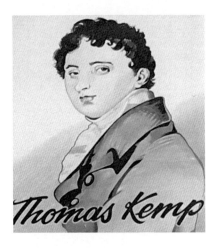

Image 8

Image 9

(Image 8) Painting of Thomas Kemp on the sign above the Thomas Kemp public house in Kemptown, 2019 by Ali Ghanimi.
(Image 9) Blue Plaque for Charles Busby in Hove, 2013 by Zigzag20s.

[...] The very wealthy bought houses, most notably the Marquis of Bristol and Lawrence Peel in the two north corners of the square and the Duke of Devonshire, at the south-west corner of Lewes Crescent. Kemp himself moved into No. 22 Sussex Square and installed his sister-in-law, Mrs. Ann Sober, next door; his brother-in-law, Philip Laycock Storey, was already established at No. 25.[13]

Thomas Kemp's pioneering building scheme – formulated in the 1820s – was too costly for him to complete, and his lack of capital caused delays. He lost his fortune and left England to get away from creditors. Yet he left a beautiful legacy – highly striking architecture in the city today.

~~~~~~~~~

Changing times: Workhouse

Perhaps because of the beauty and luxury of the Kemptown terraces, residents became protective of who should live there. This newspaper extract demonstrates how during a time of national need, people preferred to restrict occupants to the privileged few.

```
The difficulty remaining is how to house
the sick. The Guardians have fixed upon
houses in Sussex-square and Eastern-terrace
as being the only houses suitable for the
purpose. But the owners, learning that sick
people from the Workhouse were to be housed
in them, the Guardians have assured them that
no infectious cases will be brought, and that
no one in the neighbourhood will be able to
notice the presence of the patients. But so
far the owners have remained obdurate. One
hears that, failing a way out, the Guardians
will invoke the peremptory intervention
of the War Office. But they appeal to the
patriotism of the owners, whose objections
are seriously delaying the steps necessary
to prepare the Workhouse for the reception
of the Indian wounded. Surely such an appeal
will not fall on deaf ears.
```

Image 10

(Image 10) Reprinted in Blighty Brighton.
(13) The Kemp Town Estate.

Kemptown: split in two

By the 1960s, the development of Kemptown was being discussed again. The council was in favour of an extension of the dual carriageway, but this was contested by local residents. The necessity of the scheme was questioned, and the distress it caused to residents was articulated in the following newspaper clipping.

John Mogg of 5 Freshfield Place asks in QueenSpark, No. 3: Do we need to spend over £1,000,000 to extend the Eastern Road dual carriageway beyond Freshfield Road?

Extending the dual carriageway would have other disastrous consequences quite apart from the expense. More drivers would be attracted by the dual carriage way and the greater volume of traffic would bring more noise, more dirt and more danger. What madness is it to destroy homes by an unnecessary road widening scheme at a time of chronic housing shortage?

Take a look at the map below. See how the proposed road would carve its way through Kemptown. At present there's not one pedestrian crossing on the existing dual carriageway stretch and only one is being considered for the whole stretch from the Pavilion to the Marina! Kemptown is being split into two by a road no-one can cross.

The Council should abandon any ideas it has of widening Eastern Road and instead devote its energies to thinking out a complete transportation policy for this area and the whole of Brighton.

This policy should not permit the tyranny of the car to continue. It should balance the needs of the whole community and allow maximum freedom of movement for the pedestrian, commercial vehicles and the private car. Let's stop this scheme now and think again.

Image 11 (i)

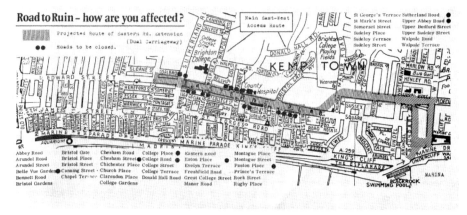

Public meeting

Only one of the 120 people who crowded into the public meeting in St. Anne's Church Hall on 7 December wanted the Eastern Road dual carriageway to be continued. The lone voice raised in support of the road widening scheme was Ald. Theobald's: he was worried about the loss of face Brighton Council would suffer if it changed its plans. He also argued that, in any case, the decision lay with the new East Sussex County Council.

Residents were not satisfied. Why couldn't Brighton Council reverse its earlier decision now? Why should homes be destroyed? What evidence was there that we needed a dual carriageway?

What use were the written assurances given by the Borough Surveyors' office that local residents would not be affected by road schemes? Why couldn't the pedestrian and the resident be considered as much as the car? Why couldn't Brighton Council have a complete transportation policy which looked after everyone's freedom of movement?

Councillor Bob Brown promised that the matter would again come before the Council. In the meantime, residents pledged their active support to the "road to ruin campaign". [14]

(Images 11 i and ii) Excerpt from QueenSpark Newsletter, p.3. Issue 3, 1973.
(14) QueenSpark Newsletter, Issue 3, 1973.

Kemptown
expansion:
demolition
of property

Just like the communities that lived within them, terraced houses relied on their neighbours for support. This newspaper clipping shows how decisions made by the council, without a proper understanding of their implications, undermined an entire row of buildings and by association, their inhabitants.

Park Street: Criminal Negligence

Nos. 1 and 2 Park Street were demolished for the widening of Eastern Road in 1970, but since No. 3 was accidentally damaged this too was razed, leaving the party wall of No. 4, owned by a nurse, Mrs Mayberry, exposed to the elements. Damp penetration was well advanced before the Council was cajoled into erecting a totally inadequate protecting wall. But this was only the beginning of Mrs Mayberry's troubles. Terraced houses support one another, and only No.1 had had a proper foundation. Mrs Mayberry's home is in an advanced state of subsidence. Cracks have appeared in all walls through which daylight can be seen. A recent architect's report described the house as in a state of imminent collapse and a danger to life. Still the Council refuses to accept any responsibility for this horrifying state of affairs and is having to be driven to Court. Alarm by residents over this, the mismanagement of the building site opposite and the miseries inflicted by the bus garage had led to the formation of a Residents Association. Secretary: Howard Barker, 23 Park Street Tel 67149

Image 13

~~~~~~~~~

Edward Street

Whereas Kemptown was a showpiece for the city, Edward Street was a dividing line between the grand terraces and the working classes trying to make ends meet.

~~~~~~~~~

Pawnbrokers

The pawnbroker was a lifeline to many families in the Edward Street area and was often referred to as the "Poor Man's Friend", but in reality was a vicious circle of poverty which few could break away from. The nickname given to our establishment was "Uncles", as was given to many pawnbrokers, probably because Mr. Lucas was considered a friend to get money from, but then the interest had to be paid on all loans, so Mr. Lucas was in a profitable business.

(Image 12 previous page) Eastern Road cutting through Sussex Square and Lewes Crescent, 1970. Royal Pavilion & Museums.
(Image 13) Excerpt from QueenSpark Newsletter, p.2. Issue 3, 1973.

The interest on a 2/6d loan was 3d (10 per cent) per week and obviously would mount up considerably if the item was not redeemed promptly.

The arrival of the rent man on a Monday would increase the number of people rushing to pawn possessions. Women very rarely held onto their wedding rings for very long and when times got hard, they would wear them into the shop, take them off and place them on the counter and then the haggling would begin. We did have a young lady who tried to pawn her engagement ring not long after her fiancé returned to the war front. She had been told that it was a family heirloom, and was obviously expecting to get a good amount of money for it. We had to inform her that it was only a Woolworth's ring and of no value at all.

Other popular items were women's boots, especially when they were the fashionably black leather patent type with white kid uppers, which could raise a good price when new, the price decreasing with the amount of visible wear. [15]

Image 14

Lucas' was the only pawnbrokers in Brighton willing to lend money against household goods as well as precious items. The shop was made up of a long narrow building on the

(Image 14) T P Lucas's pawn shop in Edward Street, c.1909.
From Christopher Horlock.
(15) At the Pawnbrokers by Lillie Morgan.

corner of Edward Street and Henry Street, situated in what was then an extremely poor part of Brighton. The shop fronting Edward Street was where goods were sold that had not been redeemed after a year in pawn. This resembled a normal type of shop, with windows covered by security bars displaying jewellery to the street, and inside household goods were displayed on shelves, with clothes and other items hanging from the ceiling.

Christmas Eve was probably one of our busiest days for Mr. Lucas always hoped to clear the shop by selling as many of the non-redeemed items as was possible, which meant that we would have to stay open until at least midnight in the hope of achieving this goal. At night all the jewellery was removed. [16]

~~~~~~~~~~

Dangers

In Edward Street during those days, you dared not walk up the road for fear of being knifed. Old women used to sit on the steps wearing long grey hair and smoking clay pipes. I have lived for only a short time in Tillstone Street but nevertheless my occupational sit-ins in various houses throughout Brighton are very vivid. [17]

(Image 15 opposite) Edward Street, Brighton, 1951. Royal Pavilion & Museums.
(16) At the Pawnbrokers by Lillie Morgan.
(17) Mrs. Barnard, Tillstone Street. QueenSpark, No.30, Winter 1982.

3: COMMUNITY LIFE IN HANOVER

WOODVALE CREMATORIUM

UPPER LEWES ROAD

LEWES ROAD

WARREN ROAD

PARK
CRESCENT

ELM GROVE

THE LEVEL

PARADE

FRESHFIELD ROAD

QUEENS PARK

DWARD STREET

ST JAMES STREET

EASTERN ROAD

ROYAL SUSSEX
HOSPITAL

MARINE PARADE

ST GEORGE'S ROAD

SUSSEX
SQUARE

Hanover Ward

Hanover is a popular residential area of brightly-painted houses on sought-after streets. It has retained its charm and character and has enjoyed regeneration, avoiding invasive redevelopment projects deployed in other parts of the city.

These streets were not so prosperous when first developed. The terraces were built rapidly from the 1860s to house an ever-expanding working community. By the end of the century, the area had been designated 'Hanover Ward', bounded by Elm Grove to the north and Sussex Street to the south.

North of Edward Street, the streets become narrower and the terraces more crowded. Home life and working life were more closely aligned with residents running businesses from home, and finding different ways to make ends meet. These extracts paint a picture of a bustling and tight-knit community.

~~~~~~~

Home and security

The house in which I spent my childhood was set in a backstreet terrace in the Hanover district of Brighton. It had no bathroom or hot water supply and only an outside loo situated at the end of a red brick path in the backyard. It meant home and security to me and my older brother Bert. We lived there with my parents and maternal grandmother. From the street three steps led up to the front door above which was a fan-light bearing a stencil reading "The Homestead".

We spent most of our time in the big basement room at the front of the house which we called the kitchen, although no cooking ever took place here to my knowledge. The range or "Kitchenor" had long since been removed and we had a lovely living coal fire for warmth. To one side of this fire stood Nan's upright Windsor armchair and to the other side an easy chair for Dad. I have no memory of a special chair for Mum. [18]

(18) Snapshots by Janis Ravenett.

Finsbury Road
School

Forget surfing the Internet, for the children of 1940s Hanover, Finsbury Road School was our window on the world. The entrance was two doors away from where we lived and I couldn't wait to be old enough to go there. Bert went a whole year ahead of me and I was green with envy. They taught him how to read and write his name and all sorts of grown-up things. He could even tie his own shoe laces – I just couldn't wait to go.

The infants' department had a separate entrance in Southover Street and to this heaven on earth my Mum was going to take me the very next morning. I can distinctly remember Bert telling me not to be nervous. He said that he would only be in the next room and if I started crying I should ask the teacher to fetch him and he would look after me. Years later I realised that this was a downright lie and teachers never fetched older brothers for any reason apart from impending death. At the time however I only wondered why on earth he thought I might cry. [19]

Image 16

(Image 16) Finsbury Road Board School, now Hanover Community Centre, c.1970. Royal Pavilion & Museums.
(19) Snapshots by Janis Ravenett.

Elm Grove

Opposite The Level are the Percy Almshouses, built in the eighteenth century, then gradually incorporated into local development schemes and eventually forming the north corner of Hanover Ward.

Image 17

~~~~~~~~~~

Elm Grove School

I commenced schooling when I was just past four years of age. One of the boys I met on that first day has remained a friend of mine ever since, and there are quite a few of my old school friends still living in the district. Elm Grove School at that time was divided into the following sections: Infants, Junior, Mixed, Senior Boys, Senior Girls. The Headmaster of the Senior Boys was a man named Mr. Mulrennan and was known by the pupils as Mouldy Lemon.

Elm Grove School was built in 1893. Pupils who reached a high standard in the 11-plus examinations went on to York Place Schools, which were the forerunner of Varndean Sixth Form College. This rule applied to all elementary schools in the Brighton area. Some who were successful were unable to take advantage of this opportunity as their parents were unable to afford the necessary uniform or support them during their stay there. With the opening of the Varndean schools the system changed. I think this was in 1928. York Place Schools

(Image 17) Percy and Wagner Almshouses, 2013 by Hassocks5489.

became the Brighton Intermediate Schools for both girls and boys. It was a sort of half-way stage between the elementary schools and Varndean School. I attended this school from 1931 to 1935.

I was pleased when I heard that my examination results enabled me to go to the Intermediate School. When I took the necessary papers home for my father to sign, he agreed to sign them only on the condition that when I left school, I would attend Evening Classes at the local Technical College. I agreed to this and subsequently attended these classes, despite attendance being interrupted by the War. I was far more successful there than I had ever been at day school. [20]

~~~~~~~~~

St. Wilfrid's

The flat where I was born was within the boundaries of the parish of St. Wilfrid's. I was christened there, and all us children went to church there, usually to the 10 o'clock children's service, and to the Sunday School in the afternoon. I believe my mother occasionally went to evensong. My parents' main Christian duties lay in providing their nine children with a loving home, and caring and providing for their every need. This left them with little time for anything else, and was no inconsiderable task. On Sundays we would put on our "Sunday Best" clothes to go to church, but immediately we returned home we took them off, hung them up, and changed into something more durable. My father was most fastidious about his own appearance, and he demanded the same standards from us. He always said that young boys had absolutely no idea of how to wear a collar and tie, they either left the top button of their shirt undone, or the knot was loose, or else the ends of the tie were flying in the breeze, or worse still the knot, instead of being secured at the throat, took up a position somewhere near the right or left ear.

To avoid such a catastrophe, we were equipped with what I can only describe as a "Choir Boy's Collar", a very wide

(20) Just one of a Large Family by Don Carter.

collar sometimes known as a celluloid or rubber collar, made of the same material as a vicar's dog collar, worn outside of our jackets rather than inside, and finished off with a bow at the throat. We hated the things, we were the only boys at church to wear them, and we stuck out like sore thumbs. The worst thing was when some "Smart Alec" sitting behind you decided to write on the collar with a pencil. So if you are of the opinion that graffiti is a modern trend, forget it. [21]

~~~~~~~

Albion Hill

Harry Cowley was one person they could always look to for a helping hand. He saw himself as something of a Good Samaritan. Indeed, religion may have increased the ardour of Harry's crusade for the dispossessed. For five years after the birth of his daughter Ruby in 1919, he "got" religion and attended church frequently. He preached Sunday services at the unemployed centre in Tichborne Street, and even had a large cross tattooed across the length and breadth of his upper body. He "lost" religion in a fight after church one day, but his campaigning speeches still often asked what Jesus would have done if he had seen the needy and unemployed of Brighton in the interwar years.

Everyone who knew Harry tells a story of "the Guv'nor's" tireless work in the neighbourhood. They remember Harry organizing outings for the poor kids of Southover Street, finding furniture for old people moved in a slum clearance, or standing up to the Board of Guardians to get more money for an out-of-luck family. [22]

In the years between the wars the Cowley family lived at 3 Grove Street, halfway up Albion Hill, in a well-established working-class community. Harry Cowley's political views were shaped by the needs of that community. Rents were high and large families crowded into the small terrace houses which ran up the hills north and east of The Level. Few breadwinners could rely on steady employment and families had to scrape and save to survive.

(21) Just one of a Large Family by Don Carter.
(22) Who was Harry Cowley?

They used their wits to find work or to get assistance from charities or the miserly Board of Guardians.

Image 18

~~~~~~~~~~

Soup kitchen

Les McLenahan grew up in the 1920s with a family of nine in two rooms on Albion Hill. His father was an invalid and his mother controlled the "Parish Purse-strings" of 27s 6d a week. "To illustrate the poverty experienced: it would mean regular patronage of the soup kitchen at Southover Street; mother sending us to Mr. Paris, the baker in Lincoln Street, for stale bread, which was soaked in the galvanized iron bath and rebaked the next day. I well remember my two brothers

(Image 18) Harry Cowley, Hyde Park, July 28, 1945, Who was Harry Cowley?

39

assisting my father to negotiate Albion Hill with the aid
of two sticks to answer 'Parish Hierarchy' questions related
to earnings he may have received through repairing boots
and shoes." [23]

~~~~~~~~

Slum clearances

In hard times people could rely on help from their neighbours,
as Molly Morley of Lincoln Street shows in her stories of
Carlton Hill before the slum clearances: "People were
borrowing from one another – tea, sugar, anything – all the
time. Mrs. Calder, at the Williams Street corner shop, used
to help people by selling them a farthing worth of tea and
ha'p'orth of sugar and milk. Street doors ever open, a hungry
child might wander and be asked, "Haven't you had any
dinner?" and answer, "No, I ain't 'ad nothin." The expected,
"Here you are then, have some of this," was a moment of joy. [24]

~~~~~~~~

Free Butt Inn

Ruby Weston, who with her husband Clem ran the Free Butt Inn
in Albion Street during the 1940s, recalls: "... poor people looked
after poor people in those days, everyone helped one another.
It doesn't occur today. And Brighton, being such a closed area
there, all up Albion Hill and Albion Street, they were all of the
same type, they were all poor people and needed help." [25]

~~~~~~~~

Ashton Street

Ashton Street originally ran south from Albion Hill. Following
a Compulsory Purchase Order it was subsequently demolished
in the slum clearance schemes.

We lived at No. 39 Ashton Street on the side farthest away
from St. Peter's Church. We had three bedrooms, but really
we only used two, the other one my grandmother used to
call a slip room, others would call it a box room. I lived
with my grandmother and mother whilst my Dad was away
at war and we didn't use the other room until the others got

(23) Who was Harry Cowley?
(24) Ibid. (25) Ibid.

back. The ground floor of the house was the old Victorian style with the passage, the sitting room where no one was allowed to go, and a room behind it where we lived and cooked on the old black range. Out at the back was a scullery with one of the old yellow stone sinks, with a copper in the corner. We had gas for cooking and electric lighting, and at the back was a little yard. You always thought if any of your friends lived in houses with bay windows they were ever so rich.

The people of Ashton Street were very friendly, and one of the things that amazes me was that at that time I can't remember anyone locking their door. If the door knocker went we either thought it was the rent man or we're in trouble, because everybody else would automatically open the door and call in, some of them would just walk in! If it rained people used to put their aspidistras out on the pavement next to the dustbins, for a watering. [26]

Image 19

(Image 19) Carlton Hill before the slum clearances, 1935.
Royal Pavilion & Museums.
(26) Back Street Brighton.

41

Carlton Hill

An area of dealers and totters: you would see them sorting their rags, and then the mums would come to find clothing and other useful items for a few pennies. There was more profit in this than when it was all weighed up for the trade. Some women would buy flour bags; these, by cutting head and arm holes, would make children's frocks, or opened up become sheets.

As families grew large this often meant moving house. Those of eleven children might also have relatives and grandparents nearby. Children called their neighbours aunts and uncle too. Although a rough area there was no necessity for locked doors. Thieves lived there but never stole in their own neighbourhood. Had one dared the wrath of a whole community would have sealed his fate! Friday nights were very tough! A man recalls seeing two women fighting down to their waists, and they each had every bit of clothing torn off them! The men just stood around. When one woman had had enough her husband pulled her out of the gutter by her hair! The police would patrol Carlton Hill "four-handed" (four at a time). There was the night in Carlton Court when about five policemen were actually knocked out by women – with fire- tongs and pokers! Their men-folk, whom the police were after, had already got clean away! [27]

Carlton Hill in 1921 was a haven for foreign refugees and immigrants. The "hokey-pokey" trade, (ice cream) was very common. I watched for hours while "Mr. Pip" Pirolli made and mixed his product.

I seemed to become aware of the words hardship and poverty. We were always hungry, or so it seemed. Looking back it must have been a nightmare for my Mum and Dad. He had been demobilised from the army and gone into the building trade as a labourer and a hod carrier. School time was always welcome, as we were always warm there, teachers understood our plight and would encourage us to run and exercise in the small playground. I hated being poor though and even now I can remember the times when we had holes in our shoes. During

(Image 20 previous page) Ashton Street, 1957. Royal Pavilion & Museums.
(27) QueenSpark, No. 6, July-Aug 1974.

prayer times in the hall, we had to kneel on the floor and I was always conscious of the state of the soles of my shoes. I never blamed my Dad for these things. How could I? I loved him very much and after all, most of the kids in our school were in the same boat.

I remember the opening of the canteen in Southover Street. Each day at school, teacher would give out tickets; one pink, one white. One ticket was for a penny and the other for five pence, old pence of course. For the penny one you were given a basin of soup and for the other five penny one you were given a roast meat dinner. My brother George had by this time started school, and we would have to take a basin or a dish to the canteen. When we collected it we would hurry home and share it between us. [28]

~~~~~~~~~

Queen's Park,
St. Luke's Terrace
School

St. Luke's School is a striking building in St. Luke's Terrace, located in the Queen's Park area of Brighton. It was built in 1903 to the design of prestigious local architect for the Brighton and Preston School Board, Thomas Simpson.

On the morning of 20th July 1903 the impressive school opened its doors for the first time. The pupils arrived from the nearby Finsbury Road School, marched in procession along St. Luke's Terrace with their books and belongings. Kathleen Back, pupil at the school from 1908, recalls her mother talking about the event, where the streets surrounding the school were full of people cheering and welcoming the pupils.

At this time, the juniors were educated separately; the Girls' Department was housed on the middle corridor with Miss Thomas as the Headmistress and the Boys' Department was located on the top corridor overseen by their Headmaster, Mr. Dewdney. They were aged between 7-14 years.

The infants' classes however, were co-educational and

(28) Backyard Brighton.

positioned on the ground floor of the school and they had as they do today, their own Head, separate entrance and playground.

During the First World War, the school was closed for a short while to serve as a hospital for Indian soldiers injured in the fighting. Fred Tester, who was at the school from 1912, remembers being sent to Elm Grove School during this time. "Seeing the school and thinking what a big place it was — being on the hill, it was open and I suppose that impressed me and when I knew that I was going there I was quite excited about it!" [29]

Image 21

Declining living conditions

Inland from Black Rock pool, you find the dense network of streets to the west of Queen's Park, built to house service workers a hundred years ago. Some of them are still rented, others have been bought on a mortgage, repaired, re-created. In Hanover Ward, one third of these houses are lived in by retired people, half of them living alone. One by one, the corner shops have closed. The church hall at the top of Islingword Road mysteriously burnt down and was rebuilt as flats by a housing association managed by a speculative developer. Places where you could meet locally for a chat, or a party, or a wedding reception have been disappearing. Nothing is taking their place. Many elderly people who

(Image 21) St Luke's School, 2010 by Hassocks5489.
(29) School Reports by past pupils of St Luke's School.

perhaps retired to Brighton and then lost their husband, wife, or friends are chronically lonely. The local response was a campaign for a community centre: Hanover Community Centre. After hesitation, support came from both Councils. [30]

~~~~~~~~~~~~

Ditchling Road

When we outgrew the bath, Mum gave us 2d to go to the Ditchling Road Baths at the corner of Rose Hill Terrace and Ditchling Road. Two of us would go together, taking our clean vest and knickers rolled in our towel with our soap and flannel. The attendant would shoot hot water through a pipe into the bath by the bucketful, according to what you had paid, and cold water was added by yourself. After bathing we washed our vests and knickers in the bath and hung them out to dry when we reached home. [31]

~~~~~~~~~~~~

Coombe Road

There was one room behind the shop in Coombe Road which was where we had our meals. There was no lounge or soft easy chairs. The room contained a large table which was scrubbed white, eight or nine chairs with hard seats, a dresser and a cabinet used for the business.

There was a large board on the wall which was used for customers' special item orders. In the corner was a hob with a kettle on all the time. The room was taken for work when it was needed. There were no radios and even conversation was scarce.

At Easter everybody mucked in for the making and packing of hot cross buns; hundreds and hundreds were made. When they were cool enough they were packed into paper bags and sold at eight for six old pence. Flour sacks were turned inside out and spread all over the floor. We were so busy at Easter that we had to eat our meals as we worked. At the end of the day we were sick of the sight of buns.

(30) Brighton on the Rocks by QueenSpark Rates Book Group.
(31) The Town Beehive by Daisy Noakes.

After the buns were baked came the big cleaning operation to get ready for making the bread. Over a usual weekend more than a thousand loaves were made, so over a holiday weekend about an extra five hundred would be required, plus brown breads like Hovis, Turog, Daren, Malt and wholemeal and also rolls and other fancy bread. [32]

~~~~~~~~~~~

Capers

My youngest brother Peter was born in 1923. Mother used to give Sam and me the job of taking him out in his pushchair, when I suppose he was about two years old. Now this pushchair was made of wood. Peter was facing the front. The pushing handle was fairly high, and Sam and I, in turn, used to get our head and shoulders through the handle, with our feet onto the axle. We were then ready to travel to the bottom of Coombe Road.

By the time we reached the bottom, we were going pretty fast. We enjoyed that, not realising the danger. This went on for quite a while. But it was on the cards that someone would go into the shop, and tell Mother what was going on. Someone did just that, so it was into deep water. Lucky for us it was Mother, and not the old man. It's daft, but capers like that stick in one's mind. [33]

(Image 22 opposite) The Cowley's home, 3 Grove Street in 1974.
Royal Pavilion & Museums.
(Image 23 next page) Hanover Terrace, 1970. Royal Pavilion & Museums.
(32) The Smiling Bakers by George Grout. (33) Ibid.

4: HOVE TERRACES

~~~~~~~

HOVE GREEN

OLD SHOREHAM ROAD

PRESTON ROAD

DYKE ROAD

NEW ENGLAND ROAD

NEW ENGLAND STREET

BUCKINGHAM PLACE

VERNON TERRACE

ST ANN'S WELL GARDENS

SURREY STREET

MONTPELIER ROAD

WESTERN ROAD

QUEENS ROAD

LAWNS

KINGSWAY

CHURCHILL SQUARE

ROYAL PAVILION

WEST STREET

KINGS ROAD

Brunswick Town

In the early part of the eighteenth century, the stylish Brunswick Square and Brunswick Terrace, 'adjacent buildings', began to take shape into a 'town' – designed by Charles Busby, who had worked on Kemp Town.

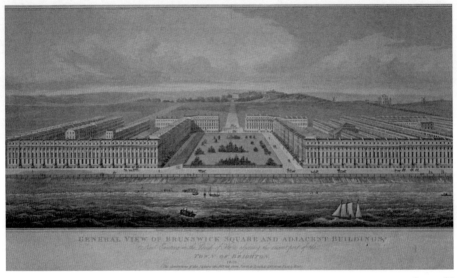

Image 24

Brunswick Town was built in the parish of Hove, but it had little impact on the existing village to the west. Instead, the new development became known as "West Brighton" reflecting its real attraction as an extension to fashionable Brighton. [34]

Substantial building work in Brunswick Town included the Italian-style St. Andrew's Church in 1827, which is located on Waterloo Street, as well as the Market and Town Halls.

~~~~~~~~~~~

Aristocrats

My father had been driving a very high-class lady, who had a summer flat in Brunswick Terrace. She was a middle-aged, very nice looking lady, with a lovely smile and such a pleasant way of speaking to you that it made you feel that the

(Image 24) Architectural view of Brunswick Square and adjacent buildings by Dubourg & Wilds, 1826. Royal Pavilion & Museums.
(34) The Regency Town House, www.rth.org

aristocrats were such delightful people: that it was all lies that they looked down their noses at the working-classes and only tolerated them because somebody had to work and keep their properties, or whatever it was they owned, clean and in order.

The lady still kept her nanny as a companion. She must have been well over 70 at that. She was very crusty and gave orders as though she was the lady and not the servant. [35]

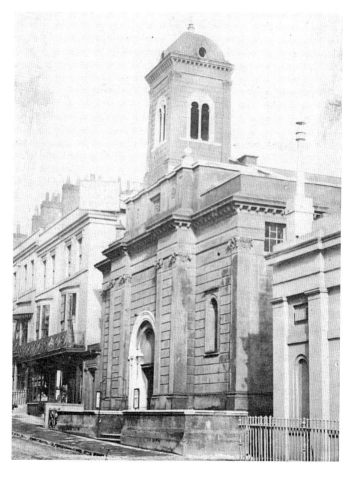

Image 25

(Image 25) St Andrew's Church, Waterloo Street. c.1890.
Royal Pavilion & Museums.
(35) Hard Times and Easy Terms by Bert Healey.

Brunswick Terrace	Brunswick Terrace when I knew it and worked it, housed well-to-do businesses, retired professionals, and titled ladies and gentlemen, with household staff, cooks, parlour maids, butlers, etc.

Now it looks like a slum – all flats, a lot empty, dilapidated.

Sometimes a little old smoothly dressed gent would hail you to take him to the bottom of West Street. He was Charlie Morton, one of the greatest racehorse trainers there was. I think he won every big race including the Derby. Several theatrical people lived along the Terrace and some titled ladies and gents, and well-known celebrities. Brunswick Terrace was Brunswick Terrace in those days [...]. [36]

~~~~~~~~~

Who was Sir Isaac Lyon Goldsmid?

[...] There have been a number of wealthy, philanthropic Jews, who, in the last century, contributed greatly to the development of Brighton and Hove, and had a wide impact on the general life of the area in local Government and trade. The first Jewish Baron, Sir Isaac Lyon Goldsmid, had the title Baron de Palmeira, bestowed on him in 1848 by the Queen of Portugal. [37]

~~~~~~~~~

Palmeira Square & Adelaide Crescent

During 1830, Isaac Goldsmid reputedly purchased 200 acres – known as the Wick Estate – in Hove, for about £60,000. He was considered a key figure in Jewish emancipation. A philanthropist and wealthy merchant banker, he was the first Jewish baronet in Britain. In an act of generosity he proffered the site upon which to build St John's Church, Hove.

He (Sir Isaac) developed Palmeira Square and Adelaide Crescent [...] Many street names in Hove are a reminder of his generosity. [38]

(36) Hard Times and Easy Terms by Bert Healey.
(37) We're not all Rothschilds! by Leila Abrahams. (38) Ibid.

WILL YOU LET ME A LOAN?

Image 26

In the service of the grand terraces

The large terraces which comprised Brunswick Town, Palmeira Square and Adelaide Crescent required a formidable workforce. Domestic service provided work for a large proportion of the city's residents. These stories give us an insight into the transition from childhood to working life: how children left school as soon as they became teenagers to get a job and, hopefully, a position to hold onto.

In the nineteenth century, domestic England ran on intensive man and horse power, both of which, having reached their peak by the end of the century, were doomed – by the First World War, the coming of the motorcar, and the changes that they brought about.

For the wealthy to live in style took a huge amount of manpower but grand housing developments were built,

(Image 26) Sir Isaac Lyon Goldsmid by Richard Dighton.
National Portrait Gallery, London.

secure in the knowledge that there was a large pool of labour available to run them.

In 1861 57% of all employed women in Sussex were domestic servants. Women in service outnumbered men by about 20 to 1. This was a period where intense poverty was found side by side with immense riches. A job in service was an opportunity for young people from large families, in which they would be not only fed, housed, trained but also receive a wage which could help support their own families.

Like the rest of Victorian society, the servants were part of a strict hierarchy. Their work was very regimented and hard. Working hours were long and time-off very rare. From the butler down to the lowly kitchen maid, each had specific tasks to accomplish.

Image 27

Contrary to modern perception, working in service was not necessarily the bed of roses that is often portrayed in the media. Discipline was strict and breaking the rules could mean instant dismissal without a reference. In fact there was a considerable flow of servants coming and going as new Agencies opened in the towns.

(Image 27) Servants of Preston Manor, c 1900 Royal Pavilion & Museums.

By the early twentieth century, wars, the invention of labour saving devices and new employment opportunities for both men and women caused a drop in servant numbers although these tended to increase during economic depressions. In consequence people started to go out to the new cafés and restaurants for meals (cheaper than employing a cook) and accelerating the changes. It became an extravagance for all but the biggest houses to have servants. [39]

~~~~~~~

Large staff

Most of the residents living there employed a large staff. There was the butler, housekeeper, nanny (if there were children), chambermaid, parlour maid, cook and the scullery maid, who was considered to be the lowest of them all, for there was even class distinction amongst the servants.

At mealtimes the butler sat at the top of the table, with the housekeeper facing him at the other end. In between the others had to sit in their set places; the scullery maid most likely in the scullery.

In the nearby mews the coachman lived over the top of the stables. These mews are now in great demand as flats. W Miles employed jobbing gardeners, landscape gardeners and tree cutters. They were employed on regular contract work in the town, spending perhaps a day or half a day in the gardens right through the year.

As driver I used to deliver their needs – tools, bedding plants and so on – and collect the garden rubbish. I used to dump this at old quarries. There were several in the town and one was off Portland Road, now Davis Park. There was one off Vale Road, now Vale Park, Portslade. We used to pay sixpence a load. [40]

(39) Servants on the Kemp Town Estate by Vanessa Minns, www.kemptownestatehistories.com
(40) A Working Man by Ernie Mason.

Image 29

~~~~~~

Kitchen maid

Mum was aptly named, Minnie Swadling, for the word "mini" suited her perfectly. A tiny woman, who even on her wedding day only weighed 7 ½ stone. She loved her surname. In the Bible it says "the child was wrapped in swaddling clothes", and at school she would say proudly, "That's my name."

Being the middle one of a family of ten children it fell to her to look after the four younger ones while her mother went out to work. It was an unbelievably difficult job for a youngster of ten years. Her father, though by no means poor, kept the family so short of money it was almost impossible to feed herself and the children. She knew little of the joys of childhood.

Release came at thirteen when Mum was sent out to service, this being one of the few occupations open to women in those days. She was sent off without even a change of underclothes.

(Image 28 previous page) The interior of a residence in King's Gardens, Hove. Royal Pavilion & Museums.
(Image 29) Old stables in Regency Mews, 2019 by Ali Ghanimi.

Fortunately the ladies' maid befriended her, and taught her how to make clothes for herself. She became an excellent needlewoman and passed on to me her love, if not the skill, of that craft. Even though she was paid only £1 a month for working hard from early morning to late at night, she was at least well fed. For some years she put up with the drudgery of being a kitchen maid, getting up at 5am to light the boiler so that the gentry were able to have hot water for their baths. [41]

~~~~~~~~~~

Housemaid

Eva was the tallest girl in the school. [...] She was fourteen years of age, had left school, and stopped working at Maxwell House and was to be trained for domestic service. [...]

Service, Eva had explained to me, was working for your living by serving other people. She said that if you were good at your work, and liked by the matron, you could be sent to a nice household where the Master and Mistress were good to their employees. She said that when you are older, if you misbehave yourself, they will not only give you a good hiding, but a lot of scrubbing and hearth stoning to do on a Saturday or Sunday afternoon. Later on I did see this happening, but not to me or my friends, thank goodness.

Eva's duties were very much full-time all the time. Each morning she cleaned and lit the dining room fire and the kitchen boiler. Then she hearth-stoned the front doorstep. After breakfast, she cleaned and swept the red carpets on the stairs and polished the brass rods and banisters. She then scrubbed the front hall and passages, and polished the hall furniture. She was very often late for dinner, but nobody took any notice. After having her meal, Eva would return to work. She often did not finish work before eight o'clock and as I went to bed at 7 o'clock, I very seldom saw her [...].

(41) Me and My Mum by Leila Abrahams, Irene Donald, June Drake, Monica Hastings, Violet Pumphery.

One night Eva came to see me when I was still awake and
I noticed how tired she looked. And when she cuddled me
her hands felt very rough. I looked at them, they were very red
and chapped with little cuts on the tips of her thumbs. [42]

~~~~~~~~

Second cook

I used to go out with some very nice girls. One particular
girl had started in service at 15, in a big house near where
I used to stand, and she worked her way up from kitchen
maid, housemaid or something, to second cook. She would
eventually be cook.

She was about 21 or so in 1928, a little bit older than me.
She was a fine, lovely girl, well-made, lovely teeth, and fair,
bobbed hair. We used to go to the pictures. She had one
full day off a month, half a day off every week, and on
Sundays, what was called an early night off. I used to meet
her mostly on her half day or Sunday evenings. I could
not manage a full day off. [43]

~~~~~~~~

Unlocked doors

I left school when I was thirteen years old and carried on
working full-time for W Miles and Company. At one time
my job was to go into rich people's houses to tend all their
plants, flowers and plumes that were in halls, dining rooms
and lounges. This meant watering and replacing many
plants and flowers. The leaves of the palms used to get
dusty and had to be sponged.

One of the houses was in King's Gardens, the residence
of Sir David Sassoon. King Edward at one time stayed
there. You cannot imagine what it was like for a poor lad
like me going into one of these houses. It was like going
into a palace, everything around was so rich and
beautiful. But what was strange was that the front doors
were always unlocked. I used to walk in and carry out
my duties and often never even saw a servant or butler.

(42) A Daughter of the State by Kathleen Dalley.
(43) Hard Times and Easy Terms by Bert Healey.

I did once go downstairs and in a small room lined with green baize met a footman cleaning a mass of silver. Such a house today would have to have an armed guard at the door! [44]

~~~~~~~~~~~

Conditions of working-class terraces

Today the majority of the existing terraced houses are modernized to accommodate twenty-first century comfort expectations. Therefore, perhaps it is easy to forget the very basic conditions of these buildings in earlier times, and how the tenants coped with their circumstances.

My earliest memories must be about the year 1910 as I was born at No. 98 Ellen Street, Hove, on 25th May, 1906. These houses have now been demolished and in their place high-rise flats have been built. No. 98 was the usual two-storeyed house. On the ground floor facing the street was the sitting room (to us it was the front room), behind was the kitchen.

The kitchen had an oven on one side of the fire, the top was for boiling and this was called the hob. The mantelpiece had a fringe tacked around it with brass-headed nails. On the wall hung a picture of the Royal Family. Dad was always for King and Country, although he had to work hard for very poor pay. We had a good doctor, who really cared for the working people, and he did not think much of Dad for voting Conservative.

Along a short passage from the kitchen was the scullery. In it, of course, were the sink, cold water tap and a coal-fired copper for boiling the dirty clothes in. At Christmas Mum boiled the Christmas pudding in it. After we had given the mixture a good stir, Dad used to put a few silver threepenny bits in it for luck. I think when Mum dished up the pudding she used to cheat a little as it was always us kids who got the threepenny pieces.

(44) A Working Man by Ernie Mason.

There was a gas cooking stove and on the wall over it was a bare gas jet. There was a very heavy mangle for wringing out the clothes after being washed. We did have a larder, but as we never had enough food to put in it, it was always full of tools and junk. We used to call it the "Black Hole", perhaps it was because having no window or light in there it was always dark.

Image 30

On Saturday evenings a galvanized bath, which usually hung on the wall in the backyard, was brought into the kitchen and placed in front of the fire. The hot water, which was heated in saucepans on top of the hob, was tipped into the bath. My eldest brother Charlie went in first. When he came out, my sister Ivy, who was a little

(Image 30) Outside toilet in backyard, Brighton, c.1935.
Royal Pavilion & Museums.

older than me, went in. Then it became my turn. A little more hot water was added each time. It was not a very big bath and the only part of our body that was covered was our bottoms.

After we had all been in the bath we had to have a dose of liquorice, which was made by mixing the powder with water. It was nasty to take, not at all like the Liquorice Allsorts we buy now.

As we got older we went to the Public Baths in Livingstone Road. We used to take our own towel and soap but we did have a real bath with lots of hot water for two pence.

The lavatory was out in the backyard separated from our neighbour by a thin wall. As you might guess, at times it was quite tuneful.

In those days most of the neighbours kept rabbits and chickens in their backyards, but not as pets – they were for food. [45]

~~~~~~~~~~

Fumigation

Our house smelt damp, musty but warm sometimes. We had bugs and had to be fumigated which left a terrible smell that took ages to go. When we came back all these bugs were lying on the floor; I thought they were ladybirds. I should imagine every house down there had some because the walls were like sponge and hardly any of the electricity worked; quite often you would put the switch on and get a shock. Once our ginger kitten was electrocuted from the bad fitting switches, and killed. [46]

~~~~~~~~~~

Goldstone Road

I was born in Hove in 1962, literally at home, which was in Wilbury Crescent as in those days planned home births were not only allowed but encouraged! I have very few clear

(45) A Working Man by Ernie Mason.
(46) Back Street Brighton.

memories of that time as my family moved away when I was four, but I distinctly remember the sounds of the nearby trains and also the frequent passing milk floats as at that time there was a nearby dairy in Davigdor Road.

After we moved my family regularly returned for the weekly Saturday shop. Our drive home frequently coincided with the end of a match at the Goldstone Ground and long before the days of instant access to such information, my father who otherwise had no interest in football would try to guess from the demeanour of the departing fans what the result might have been. He was particularly pleased if he correctly deduced from their collective expressions a nil-nil draw!

Image 31

In 1998, I moved back to Hove to a converted maisonette in Goldstone Road. The houses in the street were mostly built in the late nineteenth century and reflect in microcosm a history of social mobility and changing property prices. The terraced houses that fill the whole street were originally intended for small tradesmen and their families.

(Image 31) Goldstone Football Ground with Goldstone House in background, c.1912-14 James Gray Collection.

This was not, then, a fashionable area, but close enough to the centre of town to be convenient for those who worked there before the days of mass car ownership. I suspect that a few of the oldest present inhabitants might be the descendants of the original occupants, but for the most part the social demographic has changed out of all recognition in the last forty years, thanks to rises in property prices. The street has attracted families of young professionals and especially because of its proximity to Hove station, commuters and their families.

Many of the original terraced houses have been converted into flats and these are home to diverse social groups, in particular, to a floating population of students. With such a varied mix of people living in the same street, life is never without incident. The sound of a police siren is as common as that of an ambulance! [47]

~~~~~~~~

Brighton & Hove Albion

Brighton & Hove Albion provided a welcome relief from the pressures of the working week. The stadium was based in Hove at Goldstone Football Ground, and each week local residents would flock to the ground to support their team.

On Saturday afternoons my father and I would walk to Brighton and Hove Albion football ground and back. There were no buses along the Old Shoreham Road then. I must have been about fifteen at the time. [48]

His great interests other than the sea were his pet dogs and the Albion. He supported the Albion for over seventy years. He would have been upset at the sale of the Goldstone but I'm sure he would have travelled to see them play at Gillingham. However, I remember him best seeing him take his dog for a walk. None of his dogs wanted for exercise. On his walks he was greeted affectionately by people of all ages as what was effectively his nickname "Grandad". [49]

(47) Thoughts on Hove, Reminiscences of Daniel Kirby.
(48) A Life behind Bars by Marjory Bachelor.
(49) A Working Man by Ernie Mason.

Goldstone Street

It was due to this local support and the tenacious efforts of the fans that Goldstone Football Ground developed from a humble condition into a proper terraced structure. However, following its closure in 1997, the Goldstone Ground was demolished.

Horses were stabled round the corner in Newtown Road on Clarke's Farm. There was a large duck pond separated by a fence from the south end of the Brighton and Hove football ground (the fence being put there after the ball had to be fished out of the pond). Before the council put a sewer in Old Shoreham Road, that part behind the north end of the ground used to flood after heavy rain, so a pond appeared there sometimes. [50]

On the east side of the football ground was the residence of Mr. Clarke who owned [...] much of the ground around the area. The house was called Goldstone House. [51]

Mr Clarke (spelt also Clark) – agreed in 1926 with Chairman Charles Brown to extend the club's lease, on condition that no structure on the eastern boundary would project above the fence.

When the Albion acquired the football ground, he (John Clark) made it a condition that no stand should be built there … Goldstone House has since been demolished and there are bungalows there now. And the Albion have still not got their stand on the east side. [52]

(Image 32 opposite) Goldstone Ground, 1910. James Gray Collection.
(50) A Working Man by Ernie Mason. (51) Ibid. (52) Ibid.

5: CENTRAL
BRIGHTON

~~~~~~

TOWERS & CO. LTD.
ESTABLISHED 1881.
COLONIAL MEAT IMPORTERS
COLD STORAGE.
LONDON, SOUTHAMPTON, LIVERP

RELIANCE LAUNDRY
RECEIVING OFFICE

Clearance

In the 1950s, Brighton centre changed – there was 'slum clearance' of crammed streets of terraced houses. Russell Street and Artillery Street were destroyed, and as communities were cleared away, the Churchill Square Shopping Centre was built. Whilst conditions in the terraces could be difficult, neighbours were close and had a strong identity.

Image 34

Upper Russell Street

My family moved to 11 Upper Russell Street, in 1919. My brothers Vic and Ken were born at this house in 1921 and 1922. I was given the same name as my father who had bought a horse and cart in order to sell vegetables when he came out of the army. He then took a lock-up shop facing down Artillery Street, and became a greengrocer for a number of years.

(Image 33 previous page) Artillery Street (now Churchill Square) in 1957. View of corner with Upper Russell Street. Royal Pavilion & Museums. (Image 34) Aerial view of Churchill Square, 1973. Royal Pavilion & Museums.

Our house at 11 Upper Russell Street had been built between 1815 and 1830. The basement had railings in front of it and colonnaded arches. It was in a group of five houses which had been very well built. There was no water in the kitchen at all but there was an outhouse where there was a shallow sink, and a toilet in the back garden.

Image 35

For hot water we would boil a kettle on the range in order to wash each morning, and we bathed in a tin bath in front of the fire. There was also a dining area in the basement.

Upstairs on the ground floor we had two rooms at the front, one was used as a bedroom and one as a kind of lounge. On the top floor there were two more bedrooms.

(Image 35) Upper Russell Street, demolished in the slum clearances. Royal Pavilion & Museums.

The house was considered to be very nice, with big rooms, and although my parents only rented it, my father must have been doing quite well in order to live there. I can't remember what the rent was but I know that it was collected. We also paid rent for the shop. Our house was lit by gas to start with, but the shop had paraffin flood lamps only. [53]

~~~~~~~

Housing

Cold damp houses Rat Infestation,
Walls running wet with Condensation,
Mould growth driving us to Desperation,
Overcrowded conditions causing Degradation.

Illness is rife – we're sick through and through,
Pleurisy, Bronchitis, Coughs, Cold and 'Flu,
Asthma, Pneumonia, to name but a few,
It's hard to believe – I know – but it's true.

Brighton Council must get their priorities right,
Our homes are appalling – a terrible sight.
They're so cold it's hard to sleep in the night,
But we will not be beaten – we are ready to fight.

Improved housing we ask for – urgent action we demand,
Our good housing and good health go hand in hand,
Build us more houses – buy up more land,
The money is there – so use it!
Central Government – Be Damn'd!! [54]

~~~~~~~

Artillery Street

I lived in a small terraced house in Artillery Street. I felt a little ashamed of the address when we first moved there, as we had lived at 41 Kings Road before. My parents had worked for the owners and we only lived in, but it sounded posher.

New owners had taken over the premises in Kings Road and they had a large family so we had to move. My father still

(53) Back Street Brighton.
(54) Excerpt from QueenSpark Newletter, No. 19, Nov-Dec, Jan 1977-78.

worked for them as a House Porter and my mother sometimes cleaned, but we had to find our own accommodation.

My mother was very pleased when she found the house in Artillery Street because it had been newly decorated, but we soon found out that it was "buggy" and she just kept looking for other places to live from that day on.

The house was very small, the front door leading straight into the sitting room, the kitchen at the back and two rooms upstairs. I can't remember a bathroom, so I don't think there was one, and I suppose there was a toilet in the backyard, but I have no memory of it. [55]

The houses were strange in Artillery Street, tall, dim and smelly, all slums. My Mum used to get welfare because my Dad didn't work much. On Mondays it used to be, "Here's your Father's suit, go up the pawnshop." Or, "Take the sheets off the bed, wash them and take them along to uncle's, get a few bob till the end of the week," – which I did quite often.

We used to have to go to Royal York Buildings and get meal tickets for dinners, because they didn't give you that much money in those days, and instead gave you tickets for meals, or a pair of shoes or boots.

At Christmas we used to get little parcels; my Mum had to go and put her name down on the list to receive this. It was scrimp and scrape, and we were always on the move from one slummy house to another. It wasn't a case of 'phoning up for a removal van, we had to hire a barrow and I used to love piling everything on the barrow and helping to push it through the streets.

A lot of the houses were owned by private landlords and were quite reasonable and cheap, but if they had been taken over by the council they could have probably done something with them.

(55) Back Street Brighton.

It is a shame really they are not there anymore. Nearly every street I lived in Brighton has gone. Although they were slum areas they were happy areas. You hear lots of people say in those days you could go out and leave your front and back door open, and nobody would go in. If anyone did call in it was to say "Hello." Or, "Can I help you?" Or, "I've got the kettle on!" Even though kids had scraps and fights it didn't last or boil into anything with the neighbours. I can't see where all that understanding of the years gone by went. [56]

~~~~~~

Artillery Arms

In Artillery Street there was a public house at the top, which was run by the brothers Vine, and called the Artillery Arms.

When you went down Russell Street there was a pub half way down, which also had a gymnasium for boxers to train in. I saw Tommy Farr and Jack Pettifer, as well as most of the well known boxers of that time training there.

In that small area there must have been at least twelve pubs. There was drunkenness as the pubs opened long hours. [57]

~~~~~~

Grenville Place

I lived above my father's shop until I was married. During the war my wife took a flat in Grenville Place to be near my people, because we lived along the Gladstone Terrace, Lewes Road. They had bombs along there, and of course it worried my people, so she took a flat in Grenville Place and we were there until we had to move out.

It's not the same now. Everybody was neighbourly. Having a business you knew everyone, they all knew you and would speak to you, but you don't see a soul now. You may only see your next door neighbour sometimes. It's surprising when you move. I think business makes a great difference, people know you better then. There were all sorts of businesses down there. In Russell Street was a small boot maker; he lived at

(56) Back Street Brighton   (57) Ibid.

No. 37 and had a little business on the corner of Russell Street as it bends round. Then on the other side was a small coal merchants by the name of West; it was only a small place, but I think they used to go and get winkles, and they would sell them at sixpence a pint. I remember Milton Place, it was a rather nice area. All the streets were quite small and mainly residential. [58]

Clifton Terrace

I had been home about a week, when owing to the landlady selling the house where we were in Clifton Terrace my Father got another empty flat of three rooms, a kitchen and no

(Image 36) Grenville Place, built c.1790 and demolished in 1966.
Royal Pavilion & Museums.

(58) Back Street Brighton.

bathroom, in Port Hall Road. It had lovely big rooms,
not like the attic-type ones we had just left. I made my room
very comfortable.

There was a nice gas stove downstairs, with a 1d slot and my
Father said it would be much better if we cooked most of our
meals ourselves. It was much better than the Coffee Shop.
Food was cheap then, and I enjoyed myself cooking whatever
I fancied. [59]

~~~~~~~~~~

Sounds of the city   As the city came to life each day, its inhabitants were woken
by the familiar noises of the workers beginning their daily toil.
Vivid recollections of the sounds of the streets were captured
by the storytellers, who give an insight into the background
noise of the terraced communities.

If one is inclined to think we live in an age of noise, perhaps
they would like to cast their mind back to fifty years ago.
People were pleased to hear the hawker's cries in the street,
it meant they were really asking to do business with you. [60]

To awake very early by the clatter of milk cans being placed
on the doorstep was one of the earliest sounds. And if looking
out of the bedroom window one might see the lamplighter
extinguishing the street gas lamps he switched on overnight
by the aid of a long pole which he carries over his shoulder.

The road sweeper is busy with his broom and shovel swishing
his way along the gutters to replace the grit back on the road.
Very little rubbish was in the street, mostly horse droppings
which were collected for the gardens, or just flattened by
cartwheels passing by. The station hooter did not blast till
quarter to eight, but one could hear trains being shunted –
the freight trains being busily shunted into position in readiness
for their day's work. The steam engine pushing and pulling
the trucks seems to be protesting against the backwards and
forward movement that was expected of him. Should any

(59) Hard Times and Easy Terms by Bert Healey.
(60) Back Street Brighton.

railway worker sink back into slumber, the hooter sounded again at five minutes and at the hour.

By then all workers seemed to be on the street as the clatter of boots could be heard on the pavements. Footsteps were louder then as boots were made of leather and metal studs and pelts were nailed into the soles and heels to make them last longer.

By this time the postman would be on his rounds delivering letters and proclaiming his presence by a double rat-tat on the knocker. If a parcel was being delivered he would give a longer knock. Letters cost one penny to send and postcards one half penny. The sound of the postman's knock could be heard at quite a distance and as the sound came nearer, one waited for his familiar knock on your door. Then maybe disappointment, as the sound receded and no letter for you. [61]

~~~~~~~~

Tradesmen's traffic

Within these streets, people plied their trades, selling wares door to door. These terrace slums became not only a place to live, but a place to shop, a place to gossip, a place to mingle and a place to play.

All tradesmen's traffic was horse-drawn. The wheels of the carts had iron bands which grated on the gritty roads. Main roads were surfaced or had tar blocks, but side roads were all grit. We could sweep up some to give to our back garden chickens.

The only bad thing about the roads was when one fell over, it was a common site to see children with knees bandaged and mostly turned septic before it healed.

In summer the roads were very dusty. Then the water cart would come around. It was just a huge, square tank of water with a sprinkler the width of the tank. We children would remove our boots and socks and walk in the spray. It was a lovely sensation. [62]

(61) Street Noises by Daisy Noakes (published as Street Noises, QueenSpark Special Supplement).
(62) QueenSpark Special Supplement.

Winkle-man	The winkle-man has to work with the tide,
	When his basket is full, home he will ride,
	They are washed, and cooked, and brought round to your door
	In time for tea, who could ask for more? [63]

~~~~~~~~~

Knives and scissor grinder	At every door you'll hear him say,
	"Any knives or scissors to grind today?"
	Then works at his grindstone for a few pence.
	When work is poor, he's in suspense.
	Many doors he will call at during the day,
	Hoping in the end to get some pay. [64]

~~~~~~~~~

Rags, bottles, bones	The children on their way to school might meet the rag-and-bone man who shouted, "Rags, bottles and bones!"
	They collected all these, and also old iron. He would tell the children he would be at the school gate and if they brought any of these he would give them a windmill or balloon in exchange. Sometimes he rang a large handbell as well as shouting. [65]

~~~~~~~~~

Penny lavender	Of course, I must not forget the lady selling lavender. She would sing:
	Won't you buy my blooming lavender.
	Sixteen branches for one penny.
	At the sound of her voice my mother was out of the door, she loved lavender and our linen cupboard always smelt of it. When the clean sheets were put on the beds, it was a lovely fresh smell. It is supposed to keep moths away too.

(63) Excerpt from QueenSpark Special Supplement.
(64) Ibid. (65) Ibid.

When the new lavender was put in the linen cupboard the old was taken out and used to fumigate a sick room, by letting it smoulder in a tin lid. A little sprinkled on the hot kitchen range made a nice smell in the room. The stalks smouldered in an upright jam jar, and had the same effect. [66]

Funeral procession

Our roads must have sounded noisy in those days because when a lady lay ill, straw was strewn across the road to muffle the sound of the traffic. It stretched for several yards.

When she died, the hearse was drawn by two jet black horses and all the men wore high silk hats just as shiny black as the horses. They had black streamers and cockades on them as well. I noticed as they walked along the road how the ribbons blew in the wind.

People in the street would draw their blinds to show respect, and men raised their hats as the funeral passed. How did I know this? Because I was peeping through the curtains with my mother – the same as everyone else in the street! [67]

Image 37

(Image 37) A view of Russell Street. Royal Pavilion & Museums. (66) QueenSpark Special Supplement. (67) Ibid.

6: THE HISTORY OF WORKING LIFE IN THE CITY

WE DEMAND WINTER RELIEF.
WE WANT WORK!
WORK SCHEMES FOR BRIGHTON.

| Urban work | In addition to tradesmen offering wares, the terraced streets generated employment to those servicing the buildings themselves. The stories that follow provide an insight into the urban working environments of the working class. |

~~~~~~~

| Dustmen | The dustmen at this time had the task of digging out rubbish from dust holes and loading it into tubs, as no-one had thought of dustbins then. The flies had a lovely time, but we were not aware of contamination by flies, and they followed the collector as he emptied his load into the cart waiting in the road. |

The horses pulling these carts were large and seemed to have curly moustaches and when the driver removed the bit from their mouth so they could drink, they breathed hard on the surface of the water to remove any surface pieces.

The dustmen loved their horses, they were always well groomed and the brasses on the harness brightly polished. Some had their manes plaited with ribbons and I have seen straw hats put on their heads when the sun was extra hot. I saw one man tip a glass of beer down his horse's throat, and he thoroughly enjoyed it! [68]

~~~~~~~

| Chimney sweep | The chimney sweep was also an early riser with his brush and canes carried on his shoulder. His face already blackened with soot, but he would shout "sweep" as he walked along the road. Then anyone who needed his services could go out and book him for another day. |

Only those who lived at that time realised what a sweep's visit meant to the household. It was a terrible time. The houses were over-furnished with curtains, drapings, covers and chair backs. All this had to be removed. The venetian blinds had all to be washed as well as the little ornaments that covered the

(Image 38 previous page) Unemployed workers outside
Brighton Labour Exchange, 1939. Royal Pavilion & Museums.
(68) QueenSpark Special Supplement

mantelpiece and "what-nots". Pictures were the thing then and almost covered the walls there were so many of family portraits. These required moving and dusting behind them and glasses to be polished. The heavy carpet was taken into the garden and beaten with a carpet beater which was made of twisted cane. The plush chairs and sofa came in for a good brushing, then covered with dust sheets. Lighter furniture was removed until the sweep had gone. With the aid of a cobweb brush called "A Turk's Head", the ceiling picture rails and walls were brushed. Now all was ready for his visit.

Image 39

Don't get the idea we were idle while he was working! We would be washing and starching the white lace curtains ready to re-hang, or polishing the brass fender and fire-irons on the kitchen table, or maybe washing the ornament china, which was given as souvenirs of holidays and were very popular to have around at that time.

(Image 39) Chimney sweep John Marshall in Queen's Park Road, QueenSpark Books.

When the sweep left, no-one went into the room until the soot had settled. Then the floor was scrubbed, dust sheets removed and everything replaced. This was the usual drill for the front room or parlour which was only used on Sundays, Christmas and special occasions. Thank goodness the sweep only needed once a year for that room! The living room was much easier to cope with!

Chimney sweep rhyme:

Though blackened with soot
He never complains.
The blacker he is
The more money he gains. [69]

~~~~~~

Baker

I was working at the Brighton Co-op, doing a baker's round with a horse and cart. I was home and finished by four o'clock with five shillings a week more in my pocket. [70]

Our son George was born on May 26th, 1939, which was Whitsun Bank Holiday that year. When George was born, Dan and his friends had been to France for the day. Steamers used to go from the Palace Pier. On the Monday they arrived home to wet the baby's head. The lads arrived with their duty free champagne, a gesture which Dot and I were delighted with. Nurse Ryman, the midwife, was a grand lady who everybody knew and liked. She lived in Rose Hill Terrace but she was out all hours on her bike. Although she was strict, she had lovely ways. [71]

~~~~~~

Chair mender

I'll mend your chair, so you can use it.
I need the money, I'll not refuse it.
The seat wants re-weaving,
The woodwork a shine,
But when I've done it, you'll say, "That's fine." [72]

(69) Street Noises by Daisy Noakes.
(70) The Smiling Bakers by George Grout.   (71) Ibid.
(72) Street Noises.

Bricklayer	You left school at fourteen and started work. You never had any ambitions of doing anything except being a bricklayer, plumber or carpenter; we were trained to be craftsmen and that was that. I first started work at the age of fourteen in Sussex Street; wage five shillings, work eight in the morning to six in the evening, and eight to twelve on Saturday morning. I often had to push a handbarrow loaded with tools and ladders, there were no carts or lorries then. I was an apprentice to a place called Elliotts for four and sixpence a week in a joiners' shop.

Everyone was friendly in Jubilee Street, there were one or two of the people who lived in what we called the posher houses who weren't quite the same, but everyone seemed to get on well together. [73]

~~~~~~~~~~

Dinner ladies	Some time ago, when I was working as a school meals assistant, we had a dispute about our wages getting cut by East Sussex County Council. We were only earning £13 and it was being docked to just £8, which is an outrage when you consider what stick you took off the children.

[...] And here they were, the powers that be, coming along and just saying, "Oh, cut them dinner ladies, they are at the bottom of the tree in the school...They don't count."

"Well," I thought, "what a cheek they've got!"

They are not thinking of us as people, just as a way to save a few pounds. And not even of the children, who are to be rushed in and out of the canteen because we were to be cut in time as well.

We used to start at 12:15 – now it's 12:30 – and finish when the teachers come on duty at 1:45. Now we were to finish dead on 1:30. What we all decided to do about it was to join a union.

(73) Back Street Brighton.

So I set about after being voted in as a shop steward. I got all the girls, about nine of us, to join the union. But to my amazement, the union didn't really want to know, even despite my phone calls, and them reassuring me that everything was being done. When the head steward come down to our school one dinner time to see what exactly was going on he was amazed at the way the headmaster treated us. And at the way the kitchen staff didn't talk to us. Because the kitchen staff sent us to Coventry. They felt we were stirring things up for them and they might lose their jobs in the whiplash of things. Stupid people, I thought. We're just a small cog in a great big wheel and they are most likely to be next. Which as it turns out they are. Fighting for their jobs.

The only thing that really came out of all my efforts of phoning, and going to meetings was that the girls didn't have to work on the trolley in the canteen. It was the kitchen staff's job, which was another reason they didn't like us. It was all very, very frustrating to say the least. But the only thing that made me leave in the end was that the head was being so horrid to all the girls that they were getting fed up and leaving one by one. You can't fight alone. You have to stick together. [74]

~~~~~~~

Launderette

Image 40

(Image 40) From QueenSpark, No. 8, January-February 1975.
(74) QueenSpark Summer 1984, No. 32.

LAST WASH FOR TUDOR ?

Montreal Road Launderette.

Tudor preferred to talk to us rather than to write - so here are some of the things which came out of the conversation. By the way, as users will know, prices go up at this launderette long after elsewhere; it is clean and friendly and has a community atmosphere about it. It provokes the question in some users - why not a community-owned and run launderette as part of a community centre?

Tudor and Swarna are Buddhists. 'The good you do is God' is the basis of their beliefs, not praying for things, but being grateful. 'Religion is peace', 'gratitude is very important'. Some religions strike them as being more like businesses than true religions.

Tudor was deeply upset by the recent T.V. pictures of the Bangladesh famine. He wondered why the two helicopters shown in a programme on the famine were grounded for want of spare parts, when as soon as the Darwin disaster happened in Australia helicopters were rushed from all over the Western World.

Tudor is not a bitter person in any way, but does think that Western nations are selfish in their attitudes to mass poverty and starvation.

Image 41

~~~~~~~

Children at play

Whilst the adults were working, the children enjoyed a certain amount of freedom – once chores were completed.

We did go out to play in the street at times, when we did not have a lot of time; otherwise we went to a park. There was Preston Park which was nearest, and across the London Road, the Rookery, which is now the Rockery. [...] All was safe because there were iron fences round all the parks and gardens then. They all went for the War effort, same as people's fences round their gardens in the Second World War.

Some games we played in the street were skipping with a rope that reached the width of the road. All in together, and we could tie one end to the railing, so allowing one more to join us. [75]

As children we played in North Place and made four-wheel trucks to go down North Road in the tramlines, much to the annoyance of the tram drivers.

(Image 41) Excerpt from QueenSpark, No. 8, January-February 1975.
(75) The Town Beehive by Daisy Noakes.

My friend lived in North Road, over a shop called Bennetts, and we used to play in North Place, a cul-de-sac between Jubilee Street and the main road. We had a metal hoop, and I used to go to school running like a hare round the corner of Regent Street.

There were different seasons for toys which were popular, such as the top season. [76]

***

Wider communities and religion

Companionship was found in the terraces, on the streets, and with colleagues. City dwellers also created their own sub-communities wherever they found welcoming friends. The Church played an important role in providing comfort and practical help to its congregations. Many found support and solace in their own religious groups.

***

St. Margaret's Church

When I was old enough I went to St. Margaret's Church, which was by Regency Square, off Cannon Place. I used to go in the morning as a choir boy, to Sunday School in the afternoon, and again in the evening as a choir boy; three times every Sunday. My brothers did the same when they were old enough.

The Church of St. Margaret's was very beautiful and it had balconies all the way round where you could sit. My mother was quite religious but my father wasn't. All the children went to a Sunday School then and they always had "best" clothes to wear even if they were poor. [77]

***

Church school – St. Peter's

I went to the Central School in Church Street when I was seven, after Central Infants' School in Upper Gardner Street; it was a church school and so we had to march to St. Peter's every week.

(76) Back Street Brighton. (77) Ibid.

They also marched to Brill's Baths in Pool Valley; and as
the school had no playground they marched to Preston Park
for games lessons. We also used to go to Circus Street for
woodwork classes, that's how I became a carpenter and
joiner for the rest of my life.

They had a Sunday School at St. Peter's Church, and we went
on outings to Hassocks. We used to have to have a label tied
on us to show where we were going! Can you imagine, just for
going to Hassocks? [78]

Image 42

(Image 42) Brill's Baths in Pool Valley, Brighton. Royal Pavilion & Museums.
(78) Back Street Brighton.

Synagogues &
Jew Street

During the eighteenth century, a house on a street called 'Jew Street' became the first synagogue in Brighton. For over ten years, it was a place of worship where people could gather. The community expanded, moving to Pounes Court, and, in the early nineteenth century, to a synagogue in Devonshire Place, which held about 50 worshippers.

~~~~~~~

Middle Street

This was eventually found to be too small for the increasing population and visitors, so in 1860 No. 66 Middle Street was purchased and the architect of Brighton Station, David Mocatta, commissioned to design a building which was consecrated in September 1875. Both Middle Street and Devonshire Place are designated Grade II listed buildings.

So, from a tiny population of some 20 or so families in the eighteenth century, increasing to around 200 before the First World War, there are now approximately 2,500-3,000 families living here, some 2,000 persons being synagogue members. [79]

~~~~~~~

The tavern

Pubs offered a friendly meeting place for those in need of company.

The area around Cannon Street was full of public houses. They were the sort with sawdust on the floor so were meant for working men; you didn't get many women sitting in them. [80]

Plenty of noise is going on inside the public houses. Sounds of clinking bottles and glasses mingling with laughter and singing, which gets a bit out of time. [81]

My Grandfather kept The Black Horse in Church Street around 1860. His name was Henry James Rumble.

At the rear of the pub were some large stables. These were Royal stables associated with the Royal Pavilion.

(79) We're not all Rothschilds! by Leila Abrahams.
(80) Back Street Brighton.
(81) QueenSpark Special Supplement

My Grandfather had his own stable there [...] passing carriages stopped to drop people off for the night. Vivid memories of mine were the coaches being pulled, not only by horses, but by goats.

Beer was purchased from Tamplins (now Watneys) at the bottom of Albion Hill. I still have the trading book of 100 years ago. As a family we moved from place to place very frequently, so as to "moonlight" away from rent men and the Gadsby's Shops tallyman. If we were ever caught my Dad used to say he had a twin brother! [82]

Image 43

(Image 43) Tamplins Brewery, Brighton. Royal Pavilion & Museums.
(82) Mrs. Barnard, Tillstone Street. QueenSpark Winter 1982, No. 3.

7: BRIGHTON & HOVE
A WELCOMING CITY

Community

Despite the problems faced by residents, they were active members in their communities, and provided support to one another. Brighton & Hove has become synonymous with being an accepting and welcoming city. This openness is reflected in the archives.

~~~~~~~~~

A creative and kindly town

To find myself in Brighton, not by plan or design, and to realise my potential for homelessness, and finally live it on these welcoming streets, was an experience.

Although I was skint, scared and powerless, I had a belief in Brighton as a creative and kindly town, where humans were catered for and helped to survive. [83]

~~~~~~~~~

LGBTQ+

KAY: When I moved to Brighton from Hampstead in 1968, I came to live in Arundel Terrace. Talk about gay Brighton! It was like being back in Hampstead, in a way, except it was gayer. There was definitely a greater mix in Hampstead but here it was cliquey. If you went to one of the parties it would be mostly gay people.

TED: I found it very difficult in Southampton because I didn't really have anybody close to talk to about it, I had to cope with it on my own and it wasn't happy at times. I can remember when I was fifteen, sixteen going to bed crying and thinking I was ill and different to other people, in short, I felt very much an outcast. But when I came to Brighton [...] not knowing at that point that Brighton was the gay capital of the South Coast. Looking back on it, I suppose I felt a bit euphoric, I didn't have to conform, I could just be myself and there was no restrictions and I just dived in and never looked back. [84]

(Image 44 previous page) Brunswick Terrace, Hove, c.1950s. Royal Pavilion & Museums.
(83) Roofless.
(84) Daring Hearts.

Social progress

It is easy to forget how much times have changed. In *It's better now* the writer shows how within the timescale of one generation, some everyday hardships have been reduced.

```
It's better now

If I had lived fifty years ago, and I was very
poor, I would wear ragged clothes and I would
have no shoes and get a lot of splinters in my
feet.

I would have to work hard and I would have no
money for it. We would eat peas and potatoes,
but no fish fingers and chips. If I did get
some money, I would have to give it to my
Mum and dad.

There would be no radio and no television.
We would sit around and talk about the people
who have got a lot of money.

We would have a bowl and cold water. We would
have no washing machine. And life would be
hard.

I like it better now.
```

Image 45

~~~~~~~~

Filmmaking

The beautiful architecture and the flourishing of the city into a fashionable destination brought in photographers and filmmakers.

The old town gives a good account of herself as the gracious hostess, and whatever it was that first attracted filmmakers to these parts, the light, the architecture, the atmosphere and the local expertise, obviously still act as a lure to this day. We may no longer rival Hollywood in terms of output, and we may not have tours of film stars' homes, but a trip around our city proves that our association with cinema and celluloid has been very influential and just as enduring.

(Image 45) Kerry Ward. QueenSpark Writing, Nov. 1984.

No chapter about the history of cinema in Brighton and Hove is, of course, complete without a mention of some of the more relatively recent films that have used the city as a location. *Brighton Rock* (1947) and *Quadrophenia* (1979) may be the best remembered but there is a long list of others. Among them, *Genevieve* (1953), *Oh! What a Lovely War* (1969), *On a Clear Day You Can See Forever* (1970), *Carry On at Your Convenience* (1971), *Mona Lisa* (1986), *The End of the Affair* (1999) and *Wimbledon* (2004). There is a curious satisfaction to be had from watching these films now to see how the city has changed from decade to decade. Some would also admit to a thrill at tracing the footsteps of Barbra Streisand through the grounds of the Royal Pavilion, Kenneth Williams along Brighton Pier, or Ralph Fiennes and Julianne Moore under the arches on Madeira Drive. [85]

(Image 46 opposite) Odeon Cinema, Brighton. Royal Pavilion & Museums.
(85) Back Row Brighton.

References

QueenSpark archives

A Daughter of the State by Kathleen Dalley
A Life behind Bars by Marjory Bachelor
At the Pawnbrokers by Lillie Morgan
A Working Man by Ernie Mason
Back Row Brighton by Amy Riley, Martin Payne and Frank Flood
Back Street Brighton
Backyard Brighton
Blighty Brighton
Brighton on the Rocks by QueenSpark Rates Book Group
Daring Hearts, in collaboration with Brighton Ourstory,
    by Peter Dennis, Beccie Mannall, Linda Pointing
Hard Times and Easy Terms by Bert Healey
Just one of a Large Family by Don Carter
Me and My Mum by Leila Abrahams, Irene Donald,
    June Drake, Monica Hastings, Violet Pumphery
Oh! What a Lovely Pier by Daphne Mitchell
Roofless by various authors - Simon Brown, Chris Ellis, Mark, John Wilkins,
    Danny, Martin Curtis, Simon Nihill, Paul Budd, B, Richard Rowland
    (The Regency Project), Jacqui Martin, Mick O, Coralee, Chris, Liz Hingley,
    Jo Nean, Melissa Lee, Barry P, Wendy, Dominique De-Light
School Reports by past pupils of St. Luke's School
Snapshots by Janis Ravenett
The Book of Brighton As It Was and As It Is by Chas. H. Ross.
The Smiling Bakers by George Grout
The Town Beehive by Daisy Noakes
We're not all Rothschilds! by Leila Abrahams
Who was Harry Cowley?

Newsletters and supplements

QueenSpark Newsletter, Issue 3, 1973
QueenSpark No. 6, July-Aug 1974
QueenSpark No. 7, Oct-Nov 1974
QueenSpark No. 8, Jan-Feb 1975
QueenSpark Newletter No. 19, Nov-Dec, Jan 1977-78
QueenSpark No. 23, Summer 1979
QueenSpark No. 28, Spring-Summer 1981
QueenSpark No. 30, Winter 1982
QueenSpark No. 32, Summer 1984
QueenSpark Writing, Nov. 1984 (Kerry Ward)
QueenSpark Special Supplement
Street Noises by Daisy Noakes - QueenSpark Special Supplement

Other sources

Brighton and Hove by Nicholas Antram and Richard Morrice
Brunswick Town www.rth.org.uk
Daniel Kirby, Thoughts on Hove - submitted to Queenspark Books
Servants on the Kemp Town Estate by Vanessa Minns;
    Kemptown Histories, The Kemptown Estate
    www.kemptownestatehistories.com
The Regency Town House, The Brunswick Estate;
    Permission given by Nick Tyson www.rth.org.uk/local-history

Acknowledgements

~~~~~~

Published by QueenSpark Books, a charity
which, since 1972, has helped the people of
Brighton & Hove to tell their stories.

QueenSpark Books gratefully acknowledges
the financial assistance of The National Lottery
Heritage Fund, which made possible the
Archives Alive project, and Brighton
& Hove City Council and the University
of Brighton for their ongoing support. With
gratitude to all the volunteers and participants
in Archives Alive.

First published in Great Britain in 2019
by QueenSpark Books, Brighton, UK.

A catalogue record for this book is available
from the British Library
ISBN 978-1-9996699-5-9

Designer Emily Macaulay
www.stanleyjamespress.com

Maps by This Way
www.this-way.co

Map data by OpenStreetMap
© OpenStreetMap contributors
https://www.openstreetmap.org/copyright

Cover Illustration by Felicity Rowley

Managing Editor John Riches

Developmental Editors Kevin Bacon
(Photographs), Evlynn Sharp (Text)

Editors Jenny O'Donoghue,
Diana Varadi and James Woolley

Photo Editors Ali Ghanimi,
Natasha Gross, Terry Turner

Image archives James Gray
Collection, QueenSpark Books,
Regency Society, Royal Pavilion
and Museums, Brighton & Hove

Printed by One Digital, Woodingdean
www.one-digital.com

QueenSpark Books
www.queensparkbooks.org.uk
admin@queensparkbooks.org.uk
Registered Charity Number 1172938
Company Number 02404473